GOD
ANSWERED ME
IN TOUGH TIMES

My First Deaf Missionary Trip to Kenya, Africa in 2006

— CARL MOORE —

Inquiries and Book Orders should be addressed to:

Great Writers Media
Email: info@greatwritersmedia.com
Phone: (302) 918-5570

ISBN: 978-1-957974-05-7 (sc)
ISBN: 978-1-957974-06-4 (ebk)

Rev 3/10/2022

This book is to dedicate my parents, Rev. Carl A. Moore and Mrs. Naomi Moore, who taught me how to overcome the challenges I encountered in my life, in my disability, in my education, and in my work.

To work hard or study hard is the best way to escape boredom or become a successful person.

CONTENTS

FOREWORD BY DR. JERRY DRENNAN

CARL MOORE IS ONE OF the most prolific writers among the deaf community of the Churches of Christ.

His writings about his mission efforts throughout the world are interesting, well documented, and personal. His use of charts and photos make his topic come to life. His previous writings use the Holy Scripture to guide and help a person to achieve success with personal objectives.

I hope you, the readers, enjoy the efforts of Carl Moore as he shares this data with you.

Dr. Jerry Drennan, Emeritus
Abilene Christian University
Abilene, Texas, USA

FOREWORD BY STEPHEN GREEK

IN THE EARLY 1980S, MISSIONARIES from Abilene, Texas, visited a school for deaf children in Rongo, Kenya. They found that the school was teaching 150 students, but using no manual communication in the classrooms. The pedagogy was oriented around hearing children, with hearing teachers, yet all of the students were profoundly deaf. South 11th and Willis Church of Christ sent our family to spend two years at the school, teaching sign language to the teachers, teaching Christian religious education classes, and initiating a pilot program in which manual communication was used. The program was judged to be a success, and enthusiasm regarding Kenyan sign language began to grow. One of the criticisms of deaf education in Kenya, however, was the noticeable lack of deaf instructors. There were no deaf teachers.

Groups of missionaries began to travel to Kenya annually, always including as many hearing-impaired people as possible in the mission teams. Carl Moore joined the team traveling to Kenya in 2006 and has continued to contribute to the evangelistic effort since that first excursion to East Africa. Having a mature church leader like Carl, and an accomplished ASL teacher like his wife, Nina, has bolstered the effectiveness of this marvelous mission effort among deaf children and adults in Kenya.

In subsequent years, Carl has participated in more mission trips. He has worked with children, taught Bible classes, and ministered at several schools and orphanages serving deaf children. Carl's primary focus, however, has involved working with deaf adults. Carl has been the keynote speaker at numerous seminars designed specifically for deaf adults, both Christian and non-Christian. As a full-time minister at a deaf congregation, working with Christian leaders in the deaf churches in Kenya came quite naturally to Carl. He has taught courses specifically designed for the church leaders there. Carl's maturity as a preacher in the United States inspires deaf Christians in Kenya to pursue work in God's kingdom in similar ways.

Cross-cultural evangelism is a challenge for everyone entering a mission field. Carl's involvement in the Kenya effort continues. He has risen to the challenge. Carl continues to develop and maintain relationships with our brothers and sisters in Kenya. His love and concern for deaf people extends around the globe, embracing people of all races and nationalities. Carl's second book is a chronicle and testament to this love.

Stephen Greek, PhD
University of the Cumberlands
Williamsburg, Kentucky

PREFACE

First of all, I want to thank you, my readers. My book is a true story of my life. I hope that my book will help you with different situations in this world or by encouraging you to become a missionary like myself. More so, I want to thank to those who have supported me when I went on my mission trips for the past eight times since 2006. Also, in my book, I used the scripture text from the Easy-to-Read Version (ERV) of the Holy Bible. My goal is to encourage everyone who is deaf or hard of hearing or a hearing person to pick this version because God has a plan for our lives. More so, God provides us with all the answers in the Bible. Furthermore, I wanted to share with you about my personal experiences and how I overcame certain obstacles. Like what I said before, this is a true story of my life, and I hope that my story will touch your heart.

During my first deaf mission trip, God woke me up as He showed me what happened in other parts of this world. Since then, He changed my life. Those deaf Kenya children and adults touched my heart. While I was in Kenya, I collected some fabulous and sad stories as well as facts. In addition, I wanted to share as much as I could with you, as well as the photos I took along the way. Because of that, I went back as much as I could.

As a deaf missionary, I learned that there weren't many stories out there like mine. So, I decided to become a new author. As I shared my experiences with others through outreach efforts, I realized I could help others with my true-to-life story.

ACKNOWLEDGMENTS

I WANT TO ACKNOWLEDGE AND thank Brother Hollis Maynard, instructor, who referred me to Dr. Jerry Drennan to join with him and his Kenya Deaf Mission Team to Kenya, Africa, in 2006 so I would meet my graduation requirement at Sunset International Bible Institute (SIBI) in Lubbock, Texas.

INTRODUCTION

According to the South 11th & Willis Church of Christ, they have been participating in Summer Deaf Missions since the early 1980s. Each visit to East Africa was unique and provided glorification to our Lord Jesus Christ. Sometimes their teams were very large, sometimes they were small, depending on their objectives. Then, during the year of 2006, Carl joined with their team. Their team's name was called "Kenya Missions for the Deaf," and their goals were the following:

First goal: National deaf Christian prayer and learning workshop
Second goal: Research the possibility of establishing an orphanage home. Visit different orphanage homes' models, research different possible sites, and encourage Charles Otieno and Simeon Ongiri with this project.
Third goal: Encourage the missionaries from America.
Fourth goal: Encourage brothers and sisters in Kenya.
Fifth goal: Help us become a positive influence for world mission.

CHAPTER 1

"Give all your worries to him, because he cares for you."
(1 Peter 5:7, ERV)

CARL WENT TO KENYA, AFRICA, to meet his graduation requirement from the Sunset International Bible Institute (SIBI).

Before Carl went to Kenya, Africa, for the first time in May/June 2006, God knew about his worries (1 Peter 5:7, ERV). So, Carl prayed and asked Him to watch over him as he flew all alone from Lubbock, Texas, to Dallas, Texas, then to Chicago, Illinois.

CHAPTER 2

"The Lord is my shepherd. I will always have everything I need. He lets me lie down in green pastures. He leads me by calm pools of water. He gives new strength to my soul for the good of his name. He leads me on paths of goodness, to show he is truly good. Even if I walk through a valley as dark as the grave, I will not be afraid of any danger. Why? Because you are with me, Lord. Your rod and staff comfort me. Lord, you prepared my table in front of my enemies. You poured oil on my head. My cup is full and spilling over. Goodness and mercy will be with me the rest of my life. And I will sit in the Lord's temple for a long, long time." (Psalm 23:1–6, ERV)

As soon as Carl arrived at Chicago, Illinois, God knew about his troubles (Psalm 23:1-6, ERV). But Carl thought that everything would be all right. Well, as soon as Carl got off the plane in Chicago with escort service, this lady steward told him, "Please wait here because your plane from here in Chicago to London, England, had already left."

Carl stood there, and he became upset. Immediately, Carl knew that he was in for more trouble because he didn't bring any credit cards with him. Not only that, while Carl was in Chicago at 1:00 a.m. or 2:00 a.m. He prayed and waited for another escort service person who came and took him to the line where the airline provided him with new plane tickets, hotel, and meals.

Later, in about 2:00 a.m., when Carl finally got his hotel room, he thought that he had to go crazy to protect his money and himself. Why? Carl was carrying too much cash with him. So, he couldn't sleep well for a while.

Next day, when Carl finally got on the plane at about 3:00 p.m. from Chicago to London, he prayed that he would arrive there safely. You know Carl could not look back. He had to look forward only. So, he prayed, prayed, and prayed.

Eight hours later, Carl finally arrived at London. Then he realized that London's time was different than in the USA. So, again, he could not go to sleep. Why? Because of his money (cash), his bags, and his safety (health). Carl decided to tour the city of London by subway with all his stuff.

CHAPTER 3

"Look to God for help. You will be accepted. Don't be ashamed. This poor man called to the Lord for help. And the Lord heard me. He saved me from all my troubles." (Psalm 34:5–6, ERV)

GOD LISTENED HIS CALL FOR help. Finally, he was still safe in London. Then at about 8:00 p.m., Carl got on plane to Kenya, Africa. Again, God listened to his call for help.

"When some people have troubles they stop being proud. The Lord is close to those humble people. He will save them. Good people might have many problems, but the Lord will save them from every one of their problems." (Psalm 34:18–19, ERV)

Carl had to remind himself to stay humble and to keep on praying, praying, and praying. There Carl felt more patient with himself. He had more self-confidence and more self-control.

"Lord, hear my voice. Answer me. Be kind to me. Lord, I want to talk with you. I want to speak to you from my heart. I come before you to speak with you. Lord, don't turn away from your servant. Help me! Don't push me away! Don't leave me! My God, you are my Savior. My mother and my father left me. But the Lord took me and made me his." (Psalm 27:7–10, ERV)

You know, when you were all alone, you could say all kinds of crazy things. Well, Carl didn't. Carl prayed so often, and it helped him. Again, God listened his call for help.

> "Ropes of the grave were all around me. Traps of death lay before me. Trapped, I called to the Lord for help. Yes, I called to my God. God was in his temple. He heard my voice. He heard my cry for help." (Psalm 18:5–6, ERV)

When Carl's plane finally arrived at Kenya's airport in Kenya, Africa, around 6:30AM he was shocked to see many rebels and their jeeps all around his plane. At that moment, Carl thought that he might never come back home. Again, God listened his call for help.

CHAPTER 4

"And God's peace will keep your hearts and minds in Christ Jesus. That peace which God gives is so great that we cannot understand it." (Philippians 4:7, ERV)

AFTER HE GOT OUT OF his plane, Carl made it through the passport line on the second floor of the airport. He said to himself, "Oh boy, what a relief." Then he went downstairs to the baggage claim on the first floor. Then he was looking for Dr. Jerry Drennan, who was a group leader/interpreter from Abilene, Texas; Steve Greek, who was also a group leader/interpreter from Nashville, Tennessee; and Amos Mbithukam, who was the cab driver from Kenya. They picked him up from the airport.

After Carl got his stuff from the baggage claim, he thought, "Wow, what a blessed way of serving God's purposes."

Dr. Jerry Drennan has gone to Kenya for about twenty-three or twenty-four years when Carl first met him. Steve Greek had gone to Kenya for about eleven years. There, God gave Carl peace of mind (Philippians 4:7, ERV).

From the airport, they rode for about an hour to the guesthouse for a meeting and orientation. Not only that, Carl finally met his dream team (four deaf and three hearing adults). Carl finally slept afterward because he hasn't slept for about two days.

CHAPTER 5

"Many people are trapped and hurting because they have many troubles. Those people are crushed by the weight of their problems. Lord, be a safe place for them to run to. People who know your name should trust you. Lord, if people come to you, you will not leave them without help." (Psalm 9:9–10, ERV)

LATER, CARL'S GROUP BEGAN TO pray, meet, travel, eat, and sleep altogether daily as a team for two and a half weeks. Because of that, God protected them.

"God is our storehouse of strength. In him, we can always find help in times of trouble. So we are not afraid when the earthquakes, and the mountains fall into the sea. We are not afraid when the seas become rough and dark, and the mountains shake. SELAH." (Psalm 46:1–3, ERV)

While Carl's group traveled daily, they visited many schools for the deaf, hearing churches, deaf churches, homes, and the Kenya Deaf Christian Prayer and Learning Workshop, etc., in Kenya, Africa.

On Saturday, June 3, on their way to Nakuru Game (animal) Park, Carl's group stopped by and visited one of the schools for the deaf called Ngala School for the Deaf.

When Carl stepped out of the van, four black deaf kids approached him. They asked him, "Are you deaf and an American?"

Carl replied, "Yes, I am deaf, and I am an American."

Immediately, these kids asked him to stay right where he was. Also, these four kids ignored six white Americans (three hearing and three deaf adults) because these kids were used to seeing white hearing and white deaf adults visiting them. While Carl stood where he was, these four kids ran to the dorm, and they called other kids to come and meet him. As soon as Carl saw approximately three hundred black deaf kids run toward him, he became overwhelmed. In the meantime, these kids asked him some more questions before taking pictures in front of the Ngala School for the Deaf.

After few days, as Carl opened his Bible, he cried so hard that he felt like God challenged him to open his heart, mind, and see the world as it was. God also wanted Carl to see the bigger picture of His world. It was beyond what Carl expected to see and understand.

Carl took a lot of pictures so we could see some of it. Carl's group actually witnessed much more than what he could show to us. There were a lot of work need to be done. Back then, Carl's group did set up short-term goals and long-term goals. For example, their goals were the following:

- First goal: National deaf Christian prayer and learning workshop
- Second goal: Research the possibility of establishing an orphanage home.
  - o Visit different orphanage homes' models,
  - o research different possible sites, and
  - o encourage Charles Otieno and Simeon Ongiri with this project.
- Third goal: Encourage the missionaries from America.
- Fourth goal: Encourage brothers and sisters in Kenya.
- Fifth goal: Help us become a positive influence for world mission.

Carl's group become used to each other and become less afraid of what around them. Again, God protected them (Psalm 9:9–10; 46:1–3, ERV). This mission trip did change Carl's life. He learned like, "Are we, Christian people, doing enough?"

Later, on Thursday, June 8, Carl stopped by at Gianchere Unit (school) for the Deaf. They, Kenyan deaf children, were thrilled to see Carl, and they touched his heart. While these Kenyan deaf boys were playing soccer at Gianchere Unit for the Deaf, Carl approached them. Then Carl told them that he is an American and deaf minister. They were excited, and they asked Carl if he would come back. Carl told them that he would try his best to come back and visit them again.

CHAPTER 6

"The Lord is my shepherd. I will always have everything I need. He lets me lie down in green pastures. He leads me by calm pools of water. He gives new strength to my soul for the good of his name. He leads me on paths of goodness, to show he is truly good. Even if I walk through a valley as dark as the grave, I will not be afraid of any danger. Why? Because you are with me, Lord. Your rod and staff comfort me. Lord, you prepared my table in front of my enemies. You poured oil on my head. My cup is full and spilling over. Goodness and mercy will be with me the rest of my life. And I will sit in the Lord's temple for a long, long time." (Psalm 23:1–6, ERV)

LATER, FROM FRIDAY, JUNE 9 to Sunday, June 11, Carl went to this workshop called Kenya Deaf Christian Prayer and Learning, at Siriat Bible School in Sotik, Kenya, Africa. God watched over us (Psalm 23:1–6, ERV). These deaf Africans asked Carl to stay and live with them for good.

June 9-11, 2006
National Deaf Prayer and Learning Workshop.

Carl replied, "Thanks, but I need to go back to USA, finish my school, and get my license."

Then they asked, "Will you come back?"

"Yes, and I will try," Carl replied. More than that, in his mind, Carl said to himself, "Wow, what a heart! They really wanted him to live there with them for good." God was with them (Psalm 46:1–5, ERV).

> "God is our storehouse of strength. In him, we can always find help in times of trouble. So we are not afraid when the earthquakes, and the mountains fall into the sea. We are not afraid when the seas become rough and dark, and the mountains shake. SELAH. There is a river whose streams bring happiness to God's city, to the holy city of God Most High. God is in that city, so it will never be destroyed. God is there to help even before sunrise." (Psalm 46:1–5, ERV)

Carl believed that it was the second or third day there that he cried hard because he felt so overwhelmed that they touched his heart. So, God was with them.

CHAPTER 7

"So what should we say about this? If God is for us, then no person can stand against us. And God is with us. He even let his own Son suffer for us. God gave his Son for us all. So with Jesus now, God will surely give us all things. Who can accuse the people that God has chosen? No one! God is the One who makes his people right. Who can say that God's people are guilty? No one! Christ Jesus died [for us], but that is not all. He was also raised from death. And now he is at God's right side and is begging God for us. Can anything separate us from Christ's love? No! Can trouble separate us from Christ's love? No! Can problems or persecution separate us from Christ's love? No! If we have no food or clothes, will that separate us from Christ's love? No! Will danger or even death separate us from Christ's love? No! Like it is written in the Scriptures:

'For you [*Christ*] we are in danger of death all the time. People think we are worth no more than sheep to be killed.'

"But in all these things we have full victory through God who showed his love for us. Yes, I am sure that nothing can separate us from God's love—not death, not life, not angels or ruling spirits. I am sure that nothing now, nothing in the future, no powers, nothing above us or nothing below us—nothing in the whole created world—will ever be able to separate us from God's love that is in Christ Jesus our Lord." (Romans 8:31–39, ERV)

ALL ALONG, GOD WAS WITH them all (Romans 8:31–39, ERV), ever since in the past, present, and future. So, because of that, Carl has gone back to Kenya, Africa, eight times since 2006.

Life of Carl Moore
Revised March 27, 2020.

ABOUT THE AUTHOR

CARL WAS BORN AND RAISED in Philadelphia, PA to a deceased hearing father and deceased deaf mother. He is second oldest of seven children (three hearing and four deaf). Carl and his wife, were married in 1998 and have four grown children. Although Carl is originally from Philadelphia, PA, he has lived many places.

He is a graduate of: National Technical Institute for the Deaf/Rochester Institute of Technology (NTID/RIT) with AAS degree in Business Technology ('74), Gallaudet University (GU) with BA degree in Social Work ('81), New York University (NYU) with MA degree in Deafness Rehabilitation ('83). He also holds a Certificate of Ordination and Certification in Biblical and Deaf Ministry Studies in May 2007 and a BA degree in Biblical and Deaf Ministry Studies in May 2009 from Sunset International Bible Institute (SIBI) in Lubbock, TX.

Carl's experiences include a number of minister/counselor internships at congregations from Florida to Oklahoma, even working eight summers with a Deaf Foreign Mission Team in Kenya, Africa, between 2006 and 2017.

Carl was employed as Minister/Counselor for the Deaf/Hard of Hearing at Park Plaza Church of Christ (PPCC) Deaf Ministry in Tulsa, OK, since June 1, 2008. Then he retired on December 31, 2018, and he moved to Dallas, TX on January 26, 2019. Then he became Co-Director of Deaf Ministry on February 4, 2019 at Cedar Crest Church of Christ (CCCC) in Dallas, TX. He continued to have a great desire to reach out to the lost deaf people, hard of hearing people, and those who associate with them by sharing the Gospel of Jesus Christ with them.